valien Duyvesteyn • Dyrdahl-Roberts Family • Ron Edwards • Jennifer & Elijah Egnor • Elanore

organ Elinow • Elise • Ellie • Elliot • Emily • Emily, Benjamin & Thomas • Wyl Emsbury • Semih Energin • Ernie Engebretson • Ryker Enloe

rincess Erica • Luke Ervin • Jennie Erwin • Eryk & Erelyn • Jonah Eslinger • Esther • Ethan • Marie C.B. Evans • Tony Ewing • Ethan Fallows • Sam Farke

ll Sophia Fein • Kathy Feinstein • Moshe Ferdman • Wilhelm Fitzpatrick • Marcus Winvale Longley Fizer Funk

lexander E. Finch • Alexander Finch • Finch Family • The Fire Opal folks • Grandchild Fish • M. C. Fisher-Reid • Molly Coraline French • Freya

el Flank • Kavi Fliegel • Audelia E. Flint • Liam W. Flynn • Alice Forest • Brian Talbot Fowler • Molly Coraline French • Abby & Cooper Gar

cott Gable • Kelly Burns Gallagher • Kathy Gallucci • Mallory Galyean • Richard Gant • The Garratt Family • Abby & Cooper Gar • Gordon & Lance

Theran Jamison Gent • Dan Gerke • Chloe & Sydney Ghiringhelli • Neve Gignilliat • Diego Gil • Mathieu Gilbert • Darren • Brian Guerrero

obin Gitelman • Scout Glasgow • Michael Goff • Sarah J. Goldberg • Arthur Goldsipe • Ben & Kristine Golus • Spencer & Declan Gonzalez • Jan Groulef • Brian Guerrero

he Gornyecz Family • Grace & Ben • Aaron Grassian • Gregory • Darcy & Lilah Gresham • Griffin • Mason Danger Grouette • Emerson & Finnegan Hallihan

Dave Guin • Ernst Haeckel • Tommy Jax Halapir • Haley • Susan Hall • Violet & Dash Halliday • Emerson & Finnegan Hallihan

arris • Jonah Harrison & Arden Grace • Bjoern Hartig • Harvey • Maximus Hawkeye • Orlando Hayes • Thomas A. Hegna • Liam & Tiernan Hamill • Shala Hankison • Amy Harris

eila Jane Hekimian • Erich Wolfgang Hennig • Henry • Simon Herlihy • Deckard T Herndon • Calliope Herring • Rob Heinsoo & Lisa Eschenbach

ya Him • Jeanette & Justin Hinckley • Alistair Franklin Hiner • Wade Hlady • Grayson Lewis Hmieleski • Hobson • David Hoffman • Erin Hoffman • Marc Hertogh • Lilith Hildick • Peter C. Hildreth

ussi Hölttä • Duncan Hoogeveen • Greta & Fiona Hoffman • Emily Holder • Steve Holder • Sean Holland • Dylan Holmes • Hazel & Sadie Holmes

eegan, Piper & Hudson • Silas Hughes • River Willow Hoover • Iliana & Aurora Hopp • Elliot & Lucas Horn • Steven C Hosford • Jacqueline Hovey • Russell Hoyle

va Elizabeth Hyndman • Ilana • Shadow Hunman • Hunter • Kade Hunter • Kathren Hunter • Ben Husmann • Sahar Grace Johnston Hussain

ckson & Cara • Jaden & Bailey • Noah Iliinsky • Isa & Cora • Isabelle & Matthew • Tim "Buzz" Isakson • Liam Iverson • Mary Iverson • Ivy • IWV • Mason Jacklin

evin C Jenkins (Keovar) • Cole Thomas Jessup • Jagerson • Owen Walter James • James a.k.a. uber • Jaquette family • Jarin • Jasmine • Jasper & Owen • David Javens

arley Jo Johnston • Graham Frederick Johnston & family • Jmike • Soren John • Johnny • Kira Mae Johnson • Lorelei & Korben Johnson • Melissa Johnson

arah Kaiser • Robin Kassiday • Blaez River Jones • Jort • John Joseph • Joseph Becker • Joshua • Emily Joughin • Juliana • Juliana & Shaela

eslie Kendall • Amanda Shannon & John Kennedy • Richard & Ellen Kavanagh • Juniper & Aniko • Juniper & Carver • Mark Kadas • Max & Mara Kaehn • Metztli Kai • Kaisa & Siiri

NG TORG • Koby Kirk & Kylie Kirk • Genevieve Kitterman • Edwin Kay • Kaylee • Keegan & Riley • Kevin E Keller • Claire Kelly • Niesen & James Kelly

arie L. Knox • Michael Kohne • Jackson Komar • Darla Kennerud • Kenny • Liam Kerrigan • Loo Choo Khong • Sara Kilcher • Sungil Kim • Selita Rose Kimber

milie Krauss • Elise Kreinbring • The Krilov Family • Haley Kline • Mike Knauer • Kaidan Kneip • Aisling Knight • Ian Knight

ob Kruger • Ksenia • Elliot, Oliver & Eleanor Koziol • Aisling Knight • Ian Knight

Thanks to our backers,
who made this book possible.

Special thanks to Eric Meikle and
the other science educators who
helped us get the science right.

For Tessa, my original inspiration.   J.T.

For Kent and Sam with love.   K.L.

For more information about *Grandmother Fish* and evolution, please visit
www.GrandmotherFish.com

ISBN 978-0-9862884-0-1

This book was printed in June 2015 at Bang Printing.

First Edition
10 9 8 7 6 5 4 3 2 1

Grandmother Fish

a child's first book of Evolution
by Jonathan Tweet * illustrated by Karen Lewis

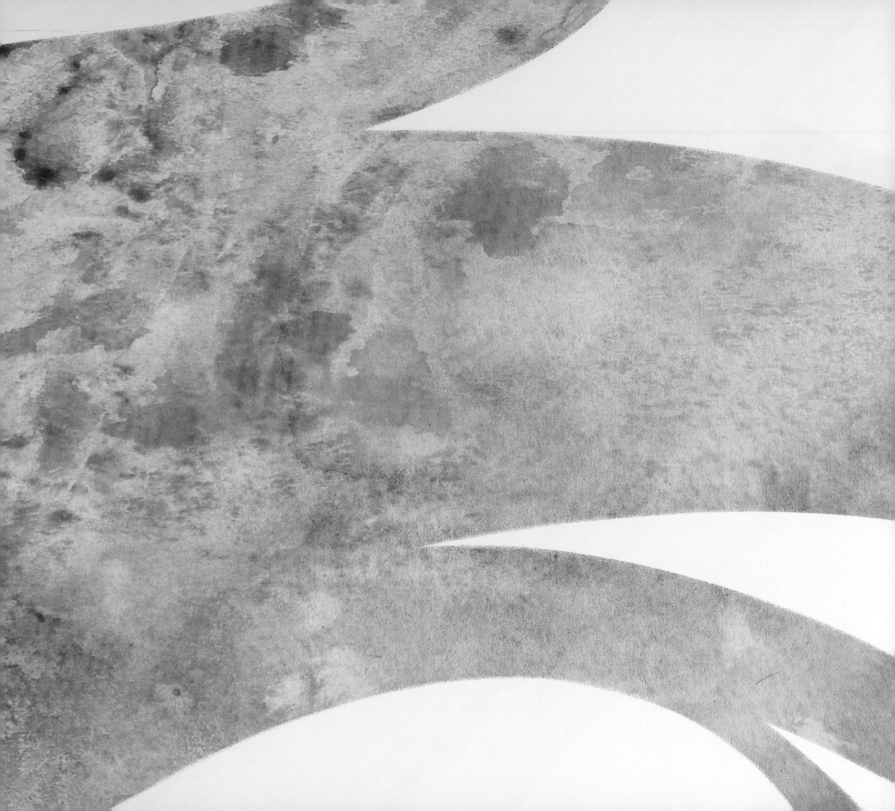

Fish

This is our Grandmother Fish.

She lived a **long, long, long, long, long** time ago.

She could **wiggle** and swim fast.

Can you wiggle?

And she had jaws to **chomp** with.

Can you chomp?

Grandmother Fish had many kinds of grandchildren.
They could **wiggle** and **chomp**.

Can you find our Grandmother Reptile?

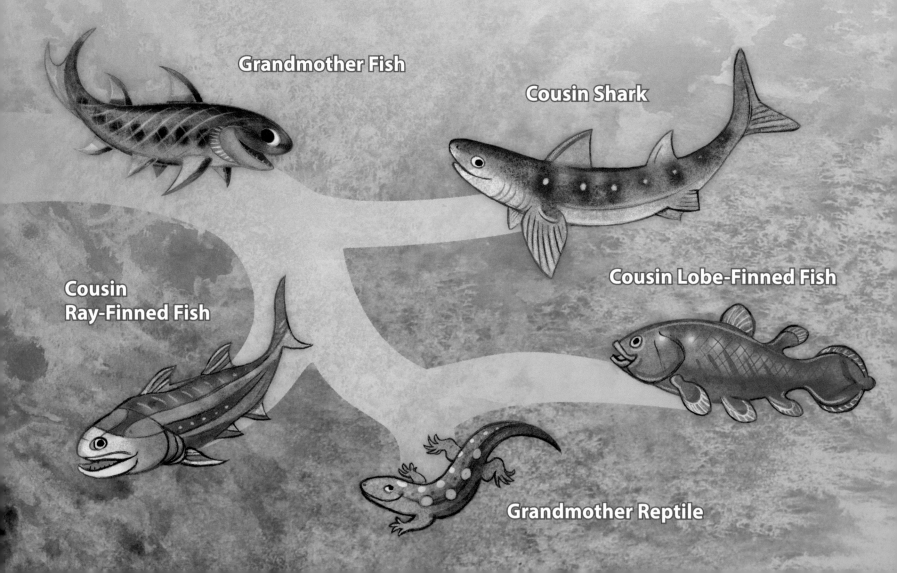

Grandmother Fish

Cousin Shark

Cousin
Ray-Finned Fish

Cousin Lobe-Finned Fish

Grandmother Reptile

Reptile

This is our Grandmother Reptile.

She lived a **long, long, long, long** time ago.

She could **crawl** across the ground.

Can you crawl?

And she could **breathe** air in and out.

Can you breathe?

Grandmother Reptile had many kinds of grandchildren.
They could **wiggle** and **chomp** and **crawl** and **breathe**.

Can you find our Grandmother Mammal?

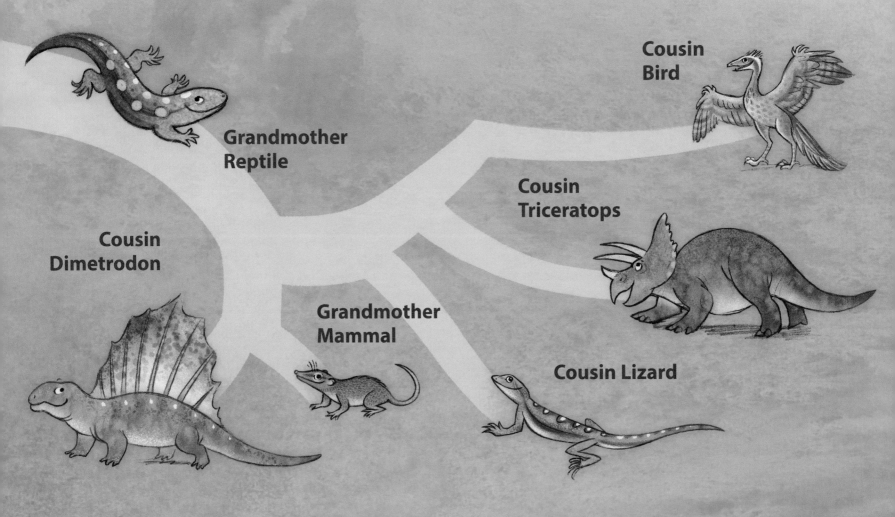

Cousin
Bird

Grandmother
Reptile

Cousin
Triceratops

Cousin
Dimetrodon

Grandmother
Mammal

Cousin Lizard

Mammal

This is our Grandmother Mammal.

She lived a **long, long, long** time ago.

Her babies could **squeak** when they were hungry.

Can you squeak?

And she could **cuddle** with her babies and feed them milk.

Can you cuddle?

Grandmother Mammal had many kinds of grandchildren. They could **wiggle** and **chomp** and **crawl** and **breathe** and **squeak** and **cuddle**.

Can you find our Grandmother Ape?

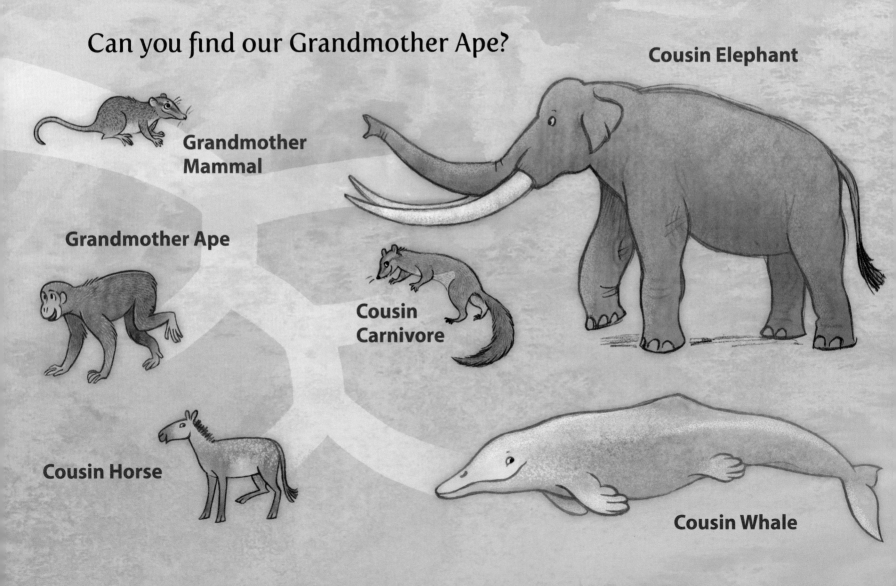

Cousin Elephant

Grandmother Mammal

Grandmother Ape

Cousin Carnivore

Cousin Horse

Cousin Whale

Ape

This is our Grandmother Ape.

She lived a **long, long** time ago.

She could **grab** branches to climb.

Can you grab?

And she could **hoot** when she was happy.

Can you hoot?

Grandmother Ape had many kinds of grandchildren.

They could **wiggle** and **chomp** and **crawl** and **breathe** and **squeak** and **cuddle** and **grab** and **hoot**.

Can you find our Grandmother Human?

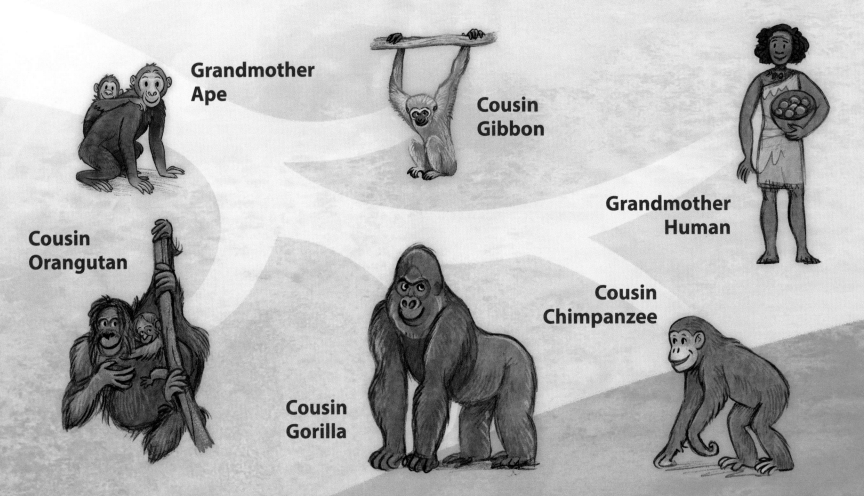

Grandmother
Ape

Cousin
Gibbon

Grandmother
Human

Cousin
Orangutan

Cousin
Chimpanzee

Cousin
Gorilla

Human

This is our Grandmother Human.

She lived a **long** time ago.

She could **walk** on two feet.

Can you walk?

And she could **talk** and tell stories.

Can you talk?

Grandmother Human had many kinds of grandchildren.
They could **wiggle** and **chomp** and **crawl** and
breathe and **squeak** and **cuddle** and **grab**

and **hoot** and **walk** and **talk** . . .

. . . and I see one of them **right here!**

Insects
Crustaceans
Horseshoe Crabs
Mollusks
Segmented Worms
Modern Sharks
Rays
Coelacanths

Flowering Plants with Seeds
Non-Flowering Plants with Seeds
grandmother fish
Early Sharks
Lobe-Finned Fishes

Ferns
Jellyfishes
Jawless Fishes
Early Ray-Finned Fishes

Green Algae
Mosses
Eels
Goldfishes
Salmon
Swordfishes

Echinoderms

ANIMALS

PLANTS

FUNGI

Mushrooms and Lichens

eukaryotes

All life on earth is related.

This family tree traces the evolution of life on earth. This tree focuses on the "Grandmothers," but the entire tree is much larger.

Put your finger on any point along any branch of this tree, and that spot represents a breeding population of living things. All the organisms further along that branch are the descendants of that population, including all the branches that branch off of it.

bacteria

archaea

Our evolutionary family tree

Modern Amphibians

Zebras

Pigs

Deer

Modern Whales

grandmother reptile

Sphenacodontids

Modern Horses

Early Whales

First Amphibians

Dolphins

Early Horses

Bats

Plesiosaurs

First Mammals

Marsupials

Bears

Lions

Snakes

Turtles

Dogs

Cats

Early Lizards

grandmother mammal

Chameleons

Crocodiles

Early Carnivores

New World Monkeys

Old World Monkeys

Pterodactyls

Early Elephants

Chimpanzees

First Dinosaurs

Ornithischian Dinosaurs

Bonobos

Saurischian Dinosaurs

grandmother ape

Gorillas

Rodents

grandmother human

Early Birds

Mammoths

Ducks

Modern Elephants

Penguins

Songbirds

Gibbons

Orangutans

Neanderthals

Dear Parents, Teachers, Babysitters, and Other Readers:

The story of *Grandmother Fish* gets children to see how evolution relates to them personally, but only you can really explain to them how evolution works. *Grandmother Fish* uses my words, but you can reach your children where they are, with your own words.

Evolution by natural selection is very difficult to understand because it doesn't make intuitive sense. Many adults have misconceptions about evolution, and to a lot of people it just doesn't make any sense at all. These last pages are for you to share with your children. They are written for you, but they are in simple terms to help you find the right words to use with your children. The simple writing also makes the material accessible to older children reading on their own.

The end notes are a resource for you to draw on when you need it. Let your children guide you in what they need to know and can understand. Skim over these back pages to see what's here, and then read whatever sections interest you or your children.

Jonathan Tweet
Seattle 2015

Explaining Concepts of Evolution

Here is a list of simple points to help you explain evolution and natural selection to children. Elaborate each point at your children's level, and explain it a little at a time.

Descent with Modification

You might also be able to point out examples of heredity and diversity in your family.

Baby animals grow up to be a lot like their moms and dads. A puppy grows up to be a dog, not a cat or a fish.

Babies grow up to be a little different from their parents. Some differences make life easier, some make life harder, and some don't matter. Differences just happen.

Over time, the differences add up, so animals today look very different from the moms and dads from a long time ago.

Artificial Selection

You can also use other examples besides dogs.

Dogs look different from how dogs used to look a long time ago.

People who wanted big dogs picked big dogs to have puppies. After a long time, their dogs were bigger than before.

Other people got different kinds of dogs, like small dogs or fluffy dogs.

All the different kinds of dogs come from one kind of dog that lived a long time ago.

Natural Selection

Natural selection works because some individuals leave many more surviving offspring than others do. Some die before reproducing, and others have few descendants for other reasons. These guidelines hint at death but don't mention it. Address the topic in ways suitable to your children.

Living in nature is dangerous for animals.

Animals have ways to keep themselves safe.

Baby animals are born with differences, and some differences make them safer. Animals that keep themselves safer have more babies.

A long time ago, one group of Grandmother Reptile's children climbed trees to be safer, and the best climbers were the safest.

The best climbers had the most babies. Those babies were also different from their parents.

After a long time, they had evolved into a kind of animal that was really good at climbing, which is Grandmother Mammal.

In different parts of the world, animals found different ways to be safe, so they evolved differently.

All the different mammals today come from one kind of mammal that lived a long time ago: Grandmother Mammal.

Guide to the Grandmothers, Their Actions, and Their Grandchildren

Grandmother Fish

Gnathostome

Our ancestors evolved into **gnathostomes** about 400 million years ago. The one pictured represents our branch of the gnathostome family tree, separate from the extinct placoderm branch.

Wiggle

They swung their tails from side to side to push themselves through the water. To wiggle like a fish, wiggle side to side.

Chomp

Jaws helped them catch and eat other animals. The other fish didn't have hinged jaws. Our ancestors could bite, but they couldn't chew.

Sharks have skeletons made of cartilage, which is lighter than bone. Ray-finned fish are almost all the fish you can think of, from sea horses to swordfish. Not many lobe-finned fish are left, unless you count the animals that descended from them: amniotes and the closely related amphibians.

Grandmother Reptile

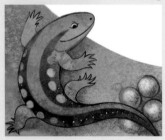

Amniote

Our ancestors evolved into **amniotes** about 300 million years ago. They laid eggs with amniotic sacs, allowing them to survive on land. Mammal children still develop in amniotic sacs.

Crawl

They crawled on their bellies, with their legs splayed out to either side, like salamanders do today.

Breathe

When they were still fish, our ancestors evolved lungs and nostrils to get more oxygen. Lungs allowed our ancestors to evolve into land animals.

Dinosaurs went extinct 65 million years ago, except for the lines that had evolved into birds. Crocodiles are closely related to dinosaurs. There are many types of lizard, some of which evolved into snakes. Before the dinosaurs evolved, Dimetrodon and related animals were top predators. We mammals are their close relatives.

Grandmother Mammal

Eutherian

Our ancestors evolved into **mammals** about 200 million years ago. The mammal pictured is a eutherian, bearing live young and nursing them like we do today.

Cuddle

They evolved cuddling as part of nursing young. Both of these behaviors are governed by the "cuddle hormone," oxytocin.

Squeak

They squeaked with the backs of their throats. We still use the throat for emotional sounds, such as laughing and crying.

After the dinosaurs died out, mammals evolved into many new forms. Elephants evolved in Africa. Like the first eutherian, the first apes and carnivores lived in the trees. Deer lived on the ground and whales in the sea. Many other types of mammals are not shown. Marsupials and monotremes are on separate lines.

Grandmother Ape

Hominoid

Our ancestors evolved into **primates** about 60 million years ago, just after the dinosaurs were wiped out. They evolved into apes about 30 million years ago.

Grab

Our early primate ancestors' paws evolved into four "hands" that helped them climb and live in trees. In humans, our rear "hands" have evolved into stable feet specialized for walking and running on the ground. They are a new kind of foot, unlike the feet of any other animal.

Hoot

Apes use their mouths as well as their throats to hoot and coo. Hooting and cooing are social activities, like squeaking. It's hard to be sure just when our ancestors started hooting.

Gibbons and orangutans live in the trees, like the first apes. Our line took to the ground, evolving into gorillas, chimpanzees, and humans. Other close relatives include bonobos and various extinct human and prehuman lines. We split from the chimpanzee line about 7 million years ago.

Grandmother Human

Homo sapiens

Our ancestors evolved into **Homo habilis** or a closely related species about 2 million years ago. "Homo" is Latin for "human," and individuals in this genus are considered human. Various other human lines evolved, and our ancestors evolved into Homo sapiens about 200,000 years ago in Africa. There were several other human species at that time, but we're the only ones left.

Walk

Our ancestors started walking on four legs over 200 million years ago. They evolved a fully bipedal stance after we split from the chimpanzee line, but millions of years before we were human.

Talk

Our whole society is based on communication and thought. Researchers disagree over when our ancestors started speaking, but probably it was between 100,000 and 500,000 years ago. Talking is an inherently social activity that would evolve only in a highly social species.

We Homo sapiens are a recent species. It has been a lot longer since the first ape than since the first Homo sapiens—150 times longer. We spent most of our time in Africa, spreading across the globe only in the last 50,000 years. We are all closely related, and we are one human race.

Correcting Common Errors
Use these notes to look for and correct any misunderstandings that your child may have.

Common Error	Instead . . .
We descended from one fish or pair of fish, or one early human or pair of early humans.	We descended from a large number of early jawed fish, and a large number of early humans. Evolution means a change in a population, not in individuals. All those early jawed fish and early humans who survived and passed their traits down to us are our ancestors.
Individual animals changed into new forms.	No individual animal changed form, such as from a fish to a reptile. Instead, children were a little different from their parents. After many generations, these differences added up, and the newer animals were different from the older ones.
Humans appeared when an ape gave birth to a human.	The differences between a parent and a child are small. Only after many generations when all the differences add up do the descendants represent a new kind of animal (or species). This book uses the friendly term "grandmother" to mean "ancestor" and "grandchild" to mean "descendant." In between "Grandmother Ape" and "Grandmother Human," there were millions of generations of intermediate "grandmothers."
Evolution progresses toward the human form.	If elephants were writing this book, it would end with Grandmother Elephant, and the elephants would think that evolution progresses toward the elephant form. Animals evolve into all sorts of new animals, and we just happen to be one of them.
Fish evolve into reptiles, reptiles evolve into mammals, and so on.	People used to think of evolution following a sequence in an upward direction, like a ladder, but that's wrong. Only one line of fish evolved into reptiles. Mostly fish have evolved into different kinds of fish. The family tree branches, so different species alive today have common ancestors in the past. Animals are still evolving today, but they are evolving in new ways, never repeating the evolution that happened long ago.
Evolution only adds traits.	Evolution also takes traits away. Whales can't crawl even though they're descended from mammals that could.
We started as fish.	We had many more ancestors before fish. This book starts with fish because very young children can relate to fish. Before our ancestors evolved into fish, they were underwater wormlike animals. The wormlike animals are also the ancestors of insects, shellfish, octopuses, and other invertebrates. When life started, it wasn't much more than organic chemicals that could make copies of themselves, and the earth was very different.
Reptiles lay eggs. Mammals give live birth.	Some reptiles give birth, and some mammals lay eggs. Children (and adults) intuitively expect simple, one-to-one relationships. But evolution makes lots of different animals, so reptiles are different from each other, and so are mammals.

Leela • Brian David Leet • Leo • Leo Bradley Kalra • Laine • J Lang • Unca Lar • Larkin • The Larsen Family • Laura • Phil, Calye, & Chance Lacefield • Ari Lacenski • Oliver Lack • Chris Lack • Fox L'Herault • Starling L'Herau... • The Kuryliv...

Liliana & Liora • Eve & Sam Lindon • Jason Lioi • Ernest Levesque • Levitan Family • Penny Lewis • The Lienau Family • Jill Lightner • Rob Lightn... • Laurel • Martin Law • New Lazzarin • L...

James & Elaine Lorenzo • Loryn & Kylie • Louisa • Daniel Loxton • Evan Loya • Joseph "Chepe" Lockett • Adele Grace Logan • Logan • Lola & Penny • Peter Lomax • Frank Lopez • Lor... • Zane Loyd • Luan • Dorit Lübke • Elizabeth Luce • Lucy • Lylah & Garrett • Lyra & Cac...

Lyra & Luca & ... • Abigail & Evelyn M. • Hugh & Ian MacDonald • Machancy • Madelief • Magus • Ruth Ellen Mahloy • Sweet Maiella • Paidia Majcher • Dr. Manda...

Kieran Manfre • Nora & Teresa Manger • Aaron, Helene, Claire & Charlie Mansheim • Bryan Manske • Aria Manzer • Benton Alexander Marchetti • Ariel Mar...

Marianna • Lindsey Marinello • Leo Marinescu • Karl Markovich • Elysia Markowitz • The Marlowe Family • Elliot Marsh • Martha & Lucas • Matthe...

Maya, Sebastian, & Caspian • Landen Reinhart Mayenfels • Jonathan Lawrence Mays • Kimbel Mazeres • Maggie McCarthy • Henry McConnell • Jeff McCo...

Anne McCrady • J McGatha & M Charlshe • Shane McGovern • Benjamin & Eleanor McKibbin • Gwendolyn McKinney • Riley Davis McLeman • Guy McLimo...

George McReynolds • João Medeiros • Xander & Avery Medvin • Garrett Meharg • Ezra Meier • Eric Meikle • Lillian Melody • Liam E Perez Mena • Jon Michae...

Uncle Mike • Evelyn Amelia Mikovich • Miranda Milburn • Miles • Benjamin Miller • Dave Miller

Karl Miller • Robert S. Miller • The Milton Girls • Miriam • Mister Pants • Lydia Mitchell • Mokona • Paula Monaghan • Eric Monkman • Shirley Monr...

Hannah, Ryan, & Sierra Moore • Joseph Moore • Katelyn Moore • Kaylee Morgan • Melissa Tiffany Morgan • Rachael L Morgan • Morgan & Ronan • Morganne...

Sean • Rowan Elizabeth Morrell • Adriana Moscatelli • Sasha Munters • Brenna Murphy • Alice "Oma" Murray • Alexander Myers • Lukas Myhan • Albert Nakar...

Andrew Thomas Nash • Nathanial • Nathicles • Allen Neil • Ada Hsu-Yin Nesse

Dana Van Nest • Nicholas & Jonathan • Dean Ernest Arthur Nicolson • Noah & Kyle • Gus Nordwall • Raven Oak • Hailey & Ayden Oepping

Nathan G.M. Ogden • Jana-Sophie Oka • Scott Okumura • Oliver & Henry • Oliver & Spencer • Olivia • Olivia • Olivia & Emmalyn • Susannah Olson-Smith • Ori...

Oriya & Serafina • Orli • Kennedy & Dylan Ortlieb • Mohi Othman • Maria & Aleksander Østby • Iridium Padfield • Fabio Milito Pagliara • Carmen & Nora Pal...

Jacob A Palmer • Neve & Erin Palmer • Maxwell Patterson • The Billy Patton Family • Lily Anne Pelley & Grandma Liz • Philip & JaVona Pepin

Morgan Perez-Mecklenborg • Missy Perritt • Noa Petel • Christina Pfaff • Phoebe • Kathryn Picard & Chris Duryee • Roy E. Plotnick • The Pohlman-Dellelo fami...

Jack Pokorny • Peter Polivka • Stephen Pollei • G & C Poole • Marie Poole • Poppy + Des Martin • Lydia Joleen Fortnam Posey • Jack, Hudson & Claire Potgiet...

Kieran Shaw Hobler Power • Inara Price • Colin Purrington • Qrab • David Quosig • Adam Rajski • Fiona & Orion Ralph • Ras • Joseph Rauscher • Loremaster Rawli...

Ryan Ray • Rachel Raymes • Darwin Alcott Redlawsk • Nobilis Reed • Reg...

Carter Reed Reichenbach • Rachel Reinfeld • Kaisa Reinikka • Tro Rex • Maayan Rezek • Althea Rice • Christopher Dale Rice • Kaitlin Rife • Neto dos R...

RJ & Elizabeth Ritter • Lester Rivera • Aviva & Aaron Robbins • Jesse Roberts • Elliott Robinson • Puck Roest • Simon Rogers • Erling W. Rog...

Mattis & Judith Rölleke • Briar Rose • Lena & Lem Rosenzweig • Jennifer A. Ross • S. Rowe • Henry Ruckdash...